# I WAS
# THAT KID

Book Cover & Layout Design: Abu Bakar Javed

Published by: DOC with TV LLC

Printed in the United States of America

ISBN: 979-8-9993418-3-9

# Dedication

For every child who has been misunderstood —
or is still being misunderstood —
know this: you can rise above any obstacle.
Do not allow circumstances or other people's
opinions to limit you.
Rise. Grow. And write your own story.

And for every adult willing to see children
differently — thank you.
Remember that your presence, your words, and
your actions matter.
They follow children longer than you may ever
realize.
They remind them who they are.
They empower them to become more.

Choose to see each child as a seed.
You may be the water, the care, or the
nourishment they need to grow.

# Table of CONTENTS

# Who This Book Is For?

This book was written for anyone who comes into contact with children — parents, educators, caregivers, mentors, and community members alike. It is an invitation to pause and reflect on how our words, actions, and attitudes can shape a child's life in ways we may never fully see.

My hope is to bring awareness, compassion, and responsibility to the role we each play in a child's journey. And for those who were once "that kid," I hope this book serves as a reminder that your beginning does not determine your ending.

You are more than what was spoken over you, and your story is still unfolding.

# INTRODUCTION

I titled this book *I Was That Kid* because I was that kid.

I was the child who didn't want to participate in gym class in elementary school. Instead of running laps or playing games, I sat in the corner reading science books, trying to figure out how to make paper from scratch so I could make money. My mind was always somewhere else — curious, thinking ahead, trying to understand the world and my place in it.

I was also a child born to a young teen mother — only seventeen years old. Life had already introduced me to realities that many children my age had not yet experienced.

In gym class, I didn't want to play. I wanted to learn. But no one took the time to ask why. No one paused long enough to see what was truly happening beneath my behavior. Instead, my gym teacher told me that I would be on welfare for the rest of my life and that I would never have anything.

Those words crushed me.

They didn't just hurt in the moment — they followed me. They walked with me through middle school, high school, and even into college. They became a quiet, lingering voice that resurfaced in moments when I needed encouragement the most.

To me, gym class felt like playtime, and at that season of my life, I wasn't interested in playing. I wish someone had taken the time to understand that participation could look different for a child like me.

Just because a child is doing something they "shouldn't" be doing does not mean that is who they will always be. Sometimes it simply means they need to be seen differently — spoken to with care — and believed in beyond their behavior.

Years later, when I was nineteen, I remember getting off the bus after work at JCPenney. I had my own apartment through the local housing authority, and as I stepped off the bus to walk home, those same words met me there again:

"You will be on welfare for the rest of your life. You will never have anything."

At that moment, I wondered if that would be true. Would I always be catching the bus? Would I ever own a car? Would my life ever look different?

There is nothing wrong with riding the bus — but at that time, I wanted more. I wanted to grow. I wanted to become the woman I felt I was meant to be.

Now, as I reflect with forgiveness and understanding, I share this story with a hope greater than my own experience. I hope it causes pause, and I hope it invites awareness. And I hope it reminds us that our words, our actions, and our presence in a child's life matter more than we may ever realize.

In this book, I invite you to reflect on how we see children, how we speak to them, how we remember them, how we support them together, and how we appreciate their differences.

My hope is that as you read, you will gently remember your own childhood — and thoughtfully consider the children whose lives you touch today.

I wanted to grow. I
wanted to become
the woman I felt I was
meant to be.

# 1

# Don't Count Me Out

*Seeing Potential Beyond the Start*

As a young child, I loved to dance and I genuinely enjoyed helping others. I could hear music playing from a mile away, and without thinking, my hips and feet would start moving to the rhythm. I was an energetic, vibrant, and joyful child—full of curiosity and life.

I remember one particular moment from my childhood that still stands out. I was participating in a relay race when the young lady I was racing alongside fell. She was nearly the size of an adult, and I was a frail ten-year-old.

When I saw her fall, I didn't think about winning the race. I ran over to her, picked her up, and carried her to the camp counselor. Winning didn't matter to me at that moment. Helping someone who had been trying her best and ended up hurt mattered far more.

That instinct—to help, to care, to look beyond myself—was already present in me at a young age.

In elementary school gym class, while my classmates were participating, I chose not to. Instead, I brought my invention books with me. One book explained how to make paper from scratch, and I was fascinated by the idea.

I thought to myself, *If I can make paper, I can sell it to my classmates. They need paper to do their work anyway.* To me, it made sense.

While the class played on one end of the gym, I sat on the floor at the other end, quietly reading. When the gym teacher noticed me, she looked over and said words that would stay with me for years:

*"You will never have anything, and you'll be on welfare for the rest of your life."*

Those words crushed me. I didn't understand why sitting and reading was seen as a problem. I didn't want to play. I wanted to learn. I wanted to create.

Now, when I look back on those moments, I can smile—not because the words didn't hurt, but because I can clearly see who that young girl really was. I see a child who loved music, loved to dance, loved helping people, and showed early signs of an entrepreneur. I can also look back with understanding toward the gym teacher.

She didn't quite see who I was, and in that moment, she had a human response: frustration took the place of patience, and unkind words replaced curiosity. What was misunderstood then now makes so much sense.

We all have moments, and I understand that raising children or working in education can be challenging. Some days require patience we feel we don't have. But we must choose not to let a child's moment become a label that counts them out. A single behavior, choice, or circumstance does not have to determine a child's future.

Sometimes, all it takes is a pause—to look beyond what a child is doing and begin to see who they are becoming.

If you work with children, raise them, teach them, or simply encounter them in your everyday life, this chapter is for you.

I understand that as a teacher, you may feel overwhelmed. Limited time, large classrooms, and repeated behaviors can wear on even the most passionate educators. In those moments, frustration can take over, leading to very human responses. I get it.

To the parent who is unsure if they are doing the right thing — I understand you too. You watch your child move through different seasons of life, and it causes you to question yourself. *Am I doing too much? Am I doing too little?* Those questions come from love.

You may also be the adult who labels behavior too quickly. I understand that as well. In the moment, frustration can rise, emotions can take the lead, and patience can slip away. On hard days, it's easy to focus on what feels disruptive, frustrating, or different.

But where a child begins does not determine where they will go.

A child's behavior in one moment does not tell the whole story of who they are. And one hard day does not define the life they are meant to live.

What if what looks like defiance is actually curiosity?

That child may simply need someone to pause for a moment and pay attention.

What if what looks like laziness is really misalignment?

 That child may need someone willing to look beyond behavior and respond without judgment.

What if what looks like a problem is actually potential looking for direction?

That child may just need someone willing to guide them.

What would happen if, instead of correcting first, we paused to ask a question?

That pause — that moment of curiosity — just might be what helps a child turn things around.

What might we discover if we chose curiosity over conclusion?

Words are powerful. They linger, they echo, and they follow children far longer than we may realize.

Potential doesn't always look polished at the start. Sometimes it looks messy, misunderstood, or inconvenient.

Seeing potential beyond the start doesn't require perfection. It simply requires willingness — the willingness to pause, to truly see, and to believe that a child's beginning is not the final word. Seeing potential is only the beginning — the words we choose next have the power to shape what a child believes about themselves, which is where the journey continues.

1. Have you ever spoken words out of frustration that you later wished you could take back? How might you approach a similar moment differently moving forward?

2. How can choosing curiosity over conclusion change the way you see and support a child?

3. Reflect on a time when someone saw potential in you beyond your circumstances. How did that impact your life, and how can you offer that same gift to a child today?

"
Seeing potential
beyond the start
doesn't require
perfection- Just
willingness!

# 2 Be Careful What You Speak

*The Power of Words*

As much as we may want to wish some of the things we've said away—or wish away words that were spoken to us—we can't. Words don't disappear. That is why it is vital that we are mindful of the words we release into the world. Once spoken, words don't get lost. They are released with purpose.

They stay, echo, and replay.

Words spoken to us in childhood—and even in adulthood—can carry lifelong weight. They can be hard to shake. As children, we often internalize words as truth. In the moment, an adult may speak something and forget it, but children remember how it made them feel. My gym teacher may not remember what she said years ago, but I remember the pain. I remember wondering if something was wrong with me.

Words spoken to children shape the internal dialogue they carry with themselves. Children are still learning and trying to navigate life, and careless words can paralyze them. Labels, once spoken, can become limitations. One word, spoken in frustration, can stay with a child much longer than we ever intend.

I remember one evening in my early twenties. It was around 9 p.m., and I was catching the bus home. After getting off the bus, I had a short walk ahead of me. As soon as my feet hit the sidewalk, those words met me—as if they had been waiting to walk home with me:

*You'll never have anything.*

I began to believe that struggle was all my life would ever be. Those words followed me through different seasons and fueled doubt within me. I had to fight against them. The battle was real.

Although those words eventually motivated me to prove them wrong, they also caused me to journey through the early parts of my life questioning myself and my future.

As I grew older and worked with children myself, I began to see just how fragile a child's heart can be. One careless word from an adult can become a story a child tells themselves for years. And one intentional word can spark hope, courage, and resilience.

Experiencing this firsthand taught me not only how deeply words can wound, but also how deeply they can heal when spoken with care.

I want to be clear—I understand. As an educator or a parent, hard days come. There are days filled with overwhelm, stress, and exhaustion. I am not expecting perfection. I served as a teacher's assistant for nearly thirteen years, so I get it. I know what it feels like to be tired. I know what it feels like to pour from an empty place.

Because of my experience, I learned the importance of speaking with awareness, patience, and purpose. I never wanted a child to hurt the way I did. I never wanted my words to limit a child in any way. Hard days are real. Emotions are real. Exhaustion is real. But words still matter.

Children should be able to look to the adults in their lives and see something worth striving toward. Even when emotions take over and something is said or done that misses the mark, take a moment to make it right.

We may not be perfect—but we can be mindful. And that effort is something children remember.

Speak encouraging words to the children in your life. Let them know they are wonderfully made. Let them know they have purpose. Let them know they will make mistakes—just like adults—but they can get back up and keep going.

Teach them not to give up. The words you speak today may become the voice they carry tomorrow. Words are seeds, released with intention, shaping how a child remembers the world and themselves.

Every word matters. Every pause matters. Every choice to encourage rather than discourage can change a child's trajectory. And sometimes, the most profound moments come not in grand speeches, but in everyday words that show care, belief, and hope.

> Consider the child who looks discouraged after a test. A simple, "I see how hard you worked," can mean more than, "You should have done better."
>
> Consider the student struggling to participate in class. A simple, "I know you can do this," can spark the courage to try again.
>
> Consider the child who feels unseen. A simple question like, "Tell me more about that," can remind them that their thoughts and feelings matter.

Every word you speak has the potential to be a seed. Some seeds may grow into doubt, others into courage. Choosing the words that nurture courage, curiosity, and confidence can transform the trajectory of a child's life.

1.  Can you recall words spoken to you as a child that still impact you today?

2.  How do you usually respond when speaking from frustration?

3.  What intentional words can you choose to speak to children moving forward?

______________________________________________________

______________________________________________________

______________________________________________________

______________________________________________________

______________________________________________________

______________________________________________________

______________________________________________________

______________________________________________________

______________________________________________________

______________________________________________________

______________________________________________________

Every word
you speak has the
potential to
be a seed!

# 3 What Will They Remember About You?

## *The Impact Adults Leave Behind*

When I think back on my childhood, there were several adults who made a lasting impact on my life. I want to take a moment to shed light on a few of them. Even small gestures from adults—words, attention, or a smile—can leave a lasting imprint on a child's life.

My middle school writing teacher was such a kind woman. I genuinely enjoyed going to her class each day. She encouraged me so much that it made me want to show up, write, and try. She would often tell me that I should consider becoming a news cast member.

I would laugh, but truthfully, it meant more to me than she probably realized. It felt good to hear someone believe in me. It made me feel smart. It made me feel like I could be something someday.

While encouragement shaped my confidence, presence shaped my sense of belonging. Another person who stands out to me from my childhood is my neighbor. He was like a grandfather to all the kids in the neighborhood.

Whenever he saw us, he would stop, tell us stories, and—most importantly—listen to us.

He was patient, answering every question we asked, no matter how silly it may have seemed. He didn't see us only for what we were doing, whether good or bad. He saw children who needed a village, and he chose to be part of that village for all of us.

There were times he would ask our parents if we could go to church with him. He would even have the church van come through the neighborhood to give us a ride. Having a relationship with Christ was vital to him, and he wanted to invite us into that same experience.

That, too, made me feel special—seen and valued.

And then there was the example I saw every day at home. I am also deeply thankful for my mother. Despite everything she faced, she pushed me to be the best version of myself from a young age. She showed me how to persevere through hard times and not give up. Her life was an example.

I watched her choose to invest in herself and go to college, even when the odds were stacked against her. Through her, I learned that impact isn't always about the words you speak—sometimes it's about the life you live in front of a child.

Each of these people impacted my life in different ways, and honestly, I am grateful for it all. Children are always watching, even when we don't think they are.

Words spoken can become a child's internal narrative for a season, and the life we live in front of them can shape who they become. Some adults helped shape who I would grow into, while others shaped what I had to heal from.

Every part of it shaped me—and in its own way, it all mattered.

My hope is that we would pause and consider who is watching us now. What version of yourself are children experiencing? Let's be mindful of the legacy we are creating. My own childhood experiences led me to want to become the kind of adult a child remembers in a positive way.

Every day we have breath is a new day filled with hope, grace, and opportunity. Because of that, it is never too late to change, to grow, and to make an impact on the children around us. Small steps matter. A shift in mindset matters.

Choosing to be present matters.

We may not be able to go back and change our childhood, but we do get to decide who someone else remembers. No one child is shaped by one adult alone. Children are shaped by families, communities, schools, churches, and everyday interactions.

This responsibility—and this opportunity—was always meant to be shared.

1. Which adults had the greatest impact on you growing up, and why?

2. Were there moments when an adult's presence—or absence—shaped how you saw yourself?

3. What do you hope someone will remember about you years from now?

We may not be able
to go back and change
our childhood, but
we do get to decide
who someone else
remembers.

# 4

# Be Their Village!

## *When Children Are Supported Together*

I remember a time in my childhood when my mom intentionally gathered a few women from our family and our neighborhood to sit with me. I was a teenager at the time, and honestly, boys were all that filled my mind. I thought I knew what I wanted, and I didn't really see why anyone needed to intervene in my life.

But my mother saw something I could not yet see. She loved me enough to invite others in.

Sitting at that table with about five women, I didn't feel attacked or judged — I felt loved. I felt seen. I felt like these women truly cared about my well-being and my future. They shared their experiences with me openly, honestly, and with compassion. They didn't talk down to me; they talked with me. And in that moment, something shifted in my heart.

That conversation pushed me to want better for myself.

Looking back now, I can say with clarity: if my village had not shown up that day, I very well could have become a young teen mom. My mother didn't try to carry everything alone — she built a circle around me, and that circle made a difference.

Not long after that, I remember going to the doctor for my annual visit. My doctor reaffirmed what my village had already shared with me. She looked me in the eyes and said, "Finish school and go to college." Those words carried weight.

They didn't land on empty ground — they landed on the foundation my village had already laid.

I thought about my own mother, who had attended college as a young woman with no childcare. I had watched her struggle, persevere, and still push forward. In that moment, I realized my village wasn't trying to control me — they were trying to protect me from a path that could slow my life down or even stop it altogether.

It took more than one adult to shape my mind and my path. I am grateful that my village chose to show up for me instead of letting me fall through the cracks.

That experience taught me something powerful: children are successful when their village shows up.

Children don't just need their parents — they need mentors, teachers, neighbors, church members, and community. Every child needs a circle of adults who care enough to be present, intentional, and aligned.

One adult's encouragement can be undone by another adult's negativity — unless the village is united. That is why a child's village must have both a mission and a vision:

A mission to show up.

A vision to see every child succeed.

Being part of a child's village does not mean doing everything. It simply means doing *something*.

Every role matters. Every voice matters. Every presence matters.

You see, my gym teacher counted me out. My neighbor welcomed me in. My mom pushed me forward. Different roles — same child. That is what a village looks like.

## The Village Protects.

A true village protects children not only physically, but emotionally. It understands that words can wound, labels can limit, and careless speech can shape a child's entire inner world.

Protection is not just about safety from harm — it is about safeguarding a child's heart.

Your presence matters to a child. Your tone matters. Your patience matters. Sometimes simply showing up is protection in itself.

## The Village Encourages.

It only takes one kind word to change the direction of a child's life. Often, it is not the grand moments that matter most — it is the small, everyday interactions.

It is the bus driver smiling as a child steps onto the bus. It is the crossing guard saying, "Have a great day."

It is the lunch lady encouraging the basketball player to eat their vegetables so they can score more in the next game.

It is the Sunday School teacher reminding children every week that they are loved, valued, and created with purpose.

Those moments may seem simple, but they plant seeds that last a lifetime.

## The Village Communicates.

When teachers and families work together, children feel secure. When families feel welcomed rather than judged, they are more likely to engage, support, and partner in their child's success.

A strong village also chooses emotional maturity. Adults must be careful not to speak negatively about children in front of them or around them. Children should never feel like they are a burden, a problem, or a disappointment.

Children should experience their village as a place of safety — not tension, conflict, or division. We were never meant to raise children in isolation. Let's not do it alone.

If you are a parent — who can you invite in to be part of your child's support system?

If you are a teacher — how can you build stronger relationships with your students' families so they truly feel like you are on the same team? In my work as a Family and Community Engagement Coordinator, I create spaces where families, educators, and community partners can come together and support students collectively. And whenever I'm in school, I try to take a moment to encourage students — simply reminding them that they are seen, capable, and smart.

If you are a neighbor, coach, or community member — how can you show up for the children around you in a meaningful way? I take every opportunity to remind the youth in my church to remember who they are and to never stop talking to God. I also volunteer when needed as the team mom on my sons' sports teams, because it gives me a chance to encourage them and their teammates that they can do it.

Every child deserves a village that sees them, believes in them, and walks with them. When a child is surrounded by a caring village, they are not only protected — they are also more likely to feel safe enough to be themselves. A strong village does not try to reshape a child into what adults prefer; instead, it makes space for who that child truly is.

Because belonging is not about fitting in — it is about being seen.

And sometimes, what children need most is not correction, but understanding.

1. Who was part of your "village" growing up? Who was missing?

2. How are you currently part of a child's village?

3. What is one intentional way you can better support children in your community?

________________________________________

________________________________________

________________________________________

________________________________________

________________________________________

________________________________________

________________________________________

________________________________________

________________________________________

________________________________________

________________________________________

________________________________________

Every child needs a circle of adults who care enough to be present, intentional, and aligned.

# 5 Appreciating Differences

*Helping Children Belong Without Changing Who They Are*

As I reflect back on my childhood, I realize I wasn't a problem child — I was simply a different kind of child. And different often makes adults uncomfortable.

In gym class, I may have come across as difficult because I didn't want to participate when my classmates were playing. Some may have viewed me as lazy because I chose to read my science books.

Others may have even labeled me rebellious. But looking back, I can clearly see the truth: I was an early thinker, a curious mind, and a creator in the making.

I wasn't trying to be difficult — I was hungry for knowledge.

In those moments, I felt out of place. While everyone else was playing, my mind was focused on learning. It wasn't that I didn't want to belong; I just wanted someone to see me — really see me. I wanted an adult to notice my curiosity, my imagination, and my desire to create.

I understand now that many adults believe children should want to play. I did enjoy playing, but I wish my gym teacher had understood that my version of engagement simply looked different. I didn't need correction — I needed understanding.

Just because a child displays differences does not mean they are defiant.

As both a former student and a classroom teacher assistant, I know that every child does not learn the same way. I remember teaching multiplication tables to my students one year. I noticed that many of them loved rap music, so instead of fighting against that, I leaned into it.

I found an instrumental beat of a song they enjoyed and had them rap their multiplication facts to the rhythm. They loved it — and honestly, so did I. Watching them learn in a way that connected to who they were confirmed something important to me: children often need different pathways to reach the same destination.

I remember a time I was teaching Sunday School. Many of the students were shy about presenting in front of others, but the pastor wanted each child to share at least once a month with the congregation. So we worked on a special assignment. I brought some supplies—aluminum foil, tape, and cardboard—and asked them to think of an object and create it with the foil, attaching it to the cardboard so it could stand.

As they worked, I spoke to them about Isaiah 64:8, reminding them that God shapes each of us for His purpose. While they molded the foil, I asked, "Did you ask the aluminum foil what it wanted to be?" They laughed and said no. I explained, "Sometimes we are like this with God—we don't understand why He made us the way He did. But we can learn to appreciate our differences, because each of us is created thoughtfully and with love."

Watching them create, laugh, and share reminded me that when children are given space to explore their unique strengths, they feel seen, valued, and empowered to grow exactly as God intended.

Not every child expresses themselves the same way. Not every child fits the traditional mold. That does not mean they are broken, behind, or less capable. They are simply being themselves — and that is not only okay, it is beautiful.

This is why it is so important that we see the child, not just the behavior. Before reacting, we must pause and ask ourselves:

What might this child need?

What could this behavior actually be revealing?

Why might they be acting this way?

Sometimes, a struggling child simply needs additional support — and that is perfectly okay. But in order to offer that support, we must be willing to listen, even when nothing is being said.

We must choose to be quick to listen and slow to respond.

If only my gym teacher had made room for my curious mind — in gym class or through another teacher. I didn't need harsh words; I needed understanding. I needed an adult who could see my heart for learning and help nurture it, even if the setting wasn't ideal.

Looking back, I wish she had connected with my mom or another teacher to build on my love of learning. The place may not have been perfect, but my passion was real — and I wish someone had caught that.

This is exactly why appreciating differences matters.

Children need adults who will not count them out, who choose their words carefully, who understand the lasting impact they leave behind, and who are willing to be part of a child's village. All of this comes together in one simple truth: children need adults who truly see them and appreciate them for who they are.

A child should never feel that they must change themselves in order to belong.

Sometimes we must meet children where they are — not where we think they should be. When children feel welcomed, valued, and supported, they grow with confidence, purpose, and hope.

When we appreciate differences, we don't just help children belong — we help them become who they were always meant to be.

1. In what ways were you different as a child? Were you accepted or misunderstood?

2. Are there children in your life that you struggle to understand? Why?

3. How can you create more space for children to be themselves without judgment?

___________________________________________

___________________________________________

___________________________________________

___________________________________________

___________________________________________

___________________________________________

___________________________________________

___________________________________________

___________________________________________

___________________________________________

A child should never
feel that they must
change themselves in
order to belong.

# PERSONAL ACTION PLAN

*Be the Adult a Child Remembers*

**Reflection Into Commitment**

**1. The Child I Need to See Differently**
Is there a specific child (or group of children) who came to mind while reading this book?

Name or describe them:

_______________________________________

_______________________________________

_______________________________________

_______________________________________

What might this child need from me that I have not fully given yet?

_______________________________________

_______________________________________

_______________________________________

_______________________________________

## 2. My Words Moving Forward

What intentional words will I choose to speak more often?

☐ "I see you."

☐ "I believe in you."

☐ "Tell me more."

☐ "You can try again."

☐ Other: ______________________________________

______________________________________


## 3. One Behavior I Will Pause Before Reacting To

What is one behavior that typically frustrates me?

______________________________________

______________________________________

______________________________________

______________________________________

What question could I ask instead of reacting immediately?

______________________________________

______________________________________

______________________________________

______________________________________

**Implementation & Accountability**

## 4. My Village Contribution

How will I intentionally show up as part of a child's village?

☐ Communicate more with families

☐ Offer encouragement daily

☐ Create space for differences

☐ Collaborate with colleagues

☐ Other: _______________________________________________

_______________________________________________

What is one specific action I will take in the next 30 days?

_______________________________________________

_______________________________________________

_______________________________________________

_______________________________________________

## 5. My Commitment Statement

Complete this sentence:

I commit to being the adult who

_______________________________

_________________________________________________________

_________________________________________________________

Signature:_______________________________

Date:_______________________________

# CLOSING — I WAS THAT KID

As you reach the end of this book, I invite you to pause and carry its message beyond these pages.

Every child has a story — some visible, some hidden. Every child carries dreams, questions, and feelings that may not always be easy to understand. But behind every behavior, every silence, every struggle, and every difference is a child who wants to be seen, valued, and believed in.

I was that kid — misunderstood, underestimated, and quietly searching for someone who would truly see me. But I was also that kid who survived, grew, learned, and became more than what was spoken over me.

And today, I stand as living proof that a child's beginning does not determine their ending.

As adults, we have the sacred responsibility and beautiful opportunity to shape how children see themselves and their world. Our words can lift or limit. Our presence can heal or harm. Our support can strengthen or weaken. And our willingness to build a village can change the trajectory of a child's life.

So I encourage you: choose curiosity over judgment, compassion over frustration, and patience over assumption. Look beyond what you see on the surface and ask what a child might need beneath it.

See every child as a seed — full of possibility, potential, and purpose.

You may be the water they need.
You may be the sunlight they need.
You may be the encouragement they need to grow.

And years from now, when that child looks back, may they remember you not as the adult who counted them out — but as the one who believed in them, stood with them, and helped them become who they were always meant to be.

Because every child deserves that kind of adult in their life.

And every child deserves a village that refuses to give up on them.